NOTES TO USERS

THESE Notes are complementary to A.P. 2095 Pilot's Notes General and assume a thorough knowledge of its contents. All pilots should be in possession of a copy of A.P. 2095 (see A.M.O. A718/48).

Additional copies may be obtained by the station publications officer by application on form 294A in duplicate, to Command Headquarters for onward transmission to A.P.F.S. (see A.P. 113). The number of the publication must be quoted in full— A.P.4308A—P.N.

Comments and suggestions should be forwarded through the usual channels to the Air Ministry (T.F.2.).

CHIPMUNK T. 10

LIST OF CONTENTS

GENERAL EQUIPMENT

PART II—HANDLING

PART III—LIMITATIONS

PART IV—EMERGENCIES

PART V—ILLUSTRATIONS

CHIPMUNK T. 10
PILOT'S CHECK LIST.

ITEM	CHECK
External checks.	
N.B. Start at the port wing root trailing edge and work clockwise around the aircraft.	
1. Port mainplane.	Condition of upper surface.
2. Port flap.	Condition and position.
3. Port aileron.	Condition. External control lock removed.
4. Port navigation light.	Condition.
5. Port mainplane.	Condition of under surface. Panels secure. Pressure-head cover removed. Fuel tank cap secure. Contents of fuel gauge. Condition of fuel vent.
6. Port undercarriage.	Security of fairing. Condition of taxying lamp. Extension of oleo leg. Brake lead secure. Tyre for cuts and creep. Chock in position.
7. Engine.	Condition of propeller and spinner. Cowlings secure. Absence of oil leaks. Condition and security of exhaust pipe.

ITEM	CHECK
8. Starboard undercarriage.	Security of fairing. Extension of oleo leg. Brake lead secure. Tyre for cuts and creep. Chock in position.
9. Starboard mainplane.	Fuel tank cap secure. Contents of fuel gauge. Condition of fuel vent. Condition of under surface. Condition of identification light. Panels secure. Security of aerial.
10. Starboard navigation light.	Condition.
11. Starboard aileron.	Condition. Security of trimming tab. External control lock removed.
12. Starboard flap.	Condition and position.
13. Starboard mainplane.	Condition of upper surface.
14. Starboard fuselage.	Condition. Panels secure.
15. Starboard tailplane.	Condition of upper and lower surfaces. Condition of leading edge.
16. Fin.	Condition. Condition of leading edge.

	ITEM	CHECK		ITEM	CHECK
17.	Starboard elevator.	Condition. Security of trimming tab. External control lock removed.	29.	Front cockpit lamps override switch.	On (down).
18.	Rudder.	Condition. Security of trimming tab. External control lock removed.	30.	Rear cockpit lamps switches.	All OFF.
19.	Tail fairing.	Condition. Condition of tail light.	31.	Ignition switches.	On.
			32.	Throttle friction nut.	Loosened.
20.	Port elevator.	Condition. External control lock removed.	33.	Direction indicator.	Caged.
21.	Port tailplane.	Condition of upper and lower surfaces. Condition of leading edge.	34.	V.H.F. change-over switch.	Front.
			35.	Muting switch.	Off (up).
22.	Tailwheel.	Extension of tailwheel strut. Tyre for cuts and creep. Valve free.	36.	Canopy.	Freedom of movement. Set half closed.

Front cockpit internal checks.

	ITEM	CHECK		ITEM	CHECK
23.	Port fuselage.	Condition. Panels secure.	37.	Control locks.	Removed and stowed.
24.	Canopy.	Security. Condition of runners. Emergency panels secure. Jettison levers flush with panels.	38.	Fire-extin-guisher.	In position.
			39.	Rudder pedals.	Adjust for length.
			40.	Flying controls.	Full and correct movement.
		N.B.—If the aircraft is to be flown solo, carry out the following checks in the rear cockpit.	41.	Amber screening.	In position or securely stowed.

Front cockpit checks.

N.B.—Switch the ground/flight switch to flight and then work from left to right.

	ITEM	CHECK		ITEM	CHECK
25.	Rear compart-ment.	No loose equipment.			
26.	Baggage locker.	Contents secure. Closed.	42.	Emergency lamp switch.	Off.
27.	Safety harness.	Secured.			
28.	Control column.	Removed (if required).	43.	Taxying lamp switch.	Off.

	ITEM	CHECK
44.	Navigation lights switch.	As required.
45.	Cockpit lamps switch.	As required.
46.	Identification light switch.	Off.
47.	Elevator trimming control.	Full and correct movement. Set to 2 divs. nose heavy.
48.	Brake lever.	Freedom of movement. Set fully on.
49.	Mixture control.	Fully rich.
50.	Throttle.	Freedom of movement. Closed. Adjust friction.
51.	Ignition switches.	Off.
52.	Generator power failure warning light.	On.
53.	Direction indicator.	Caged
54.	V.H.F. controller.	Off.
55.	Magnetic compass.	Serviceability. Lamp switch as required.
56.	Fuel cock.	On.
57.	Flap lever.	Operation. Check with flaps position. Flaps up.
58.	Carburettor air intake control.	Freedom of movement. Set to cold.

	ITEM	CHECK
	Start and warm up the engine (see para. 25).	
59.	Direction indicator.	Set with magnetic compass. Uncage.
60.	Radio.	Test V.H.F. Check altimeter setting with control.
	Exercise and test the engine (see para. 26).	
61.	Chocks.	Clear.
62.	Brake lever.	About half on.
63.	Taxying.	As soon as possible test brakes. Direction indicator for accuracy. Artificial horizon for accuracy. Check temperatures and pressures.
	Checks before take-off.	
64.	Trim— Elevator.	2 divs. nose heavy.
65.	Mixture.	Fully rich.
66.	Throttle friction.	Adjust.
67.	Carburettor air intake.	As required.
68.	Fuel.	Contents. Cock on.
69.	Flaps.	Up. 15° down for shortest run.
70.	Harness.	Tight.
	Checks in flight as necessary.	
	Checks before landing—reduce speed to 75 knots.	
71.	Harness.	Tight.
72.	Fuel.	Contents.
73.	Mixture.	Fully rich.

	ITEM	CHECK		ITEM	CHECK
74.	Carburettor air intake.	As required.	81.	Fuel cock.	Off.
			82.	Electrical services.	All off.
75.	Flaps.	As required.			
	After landing.—Clear runway.		83.	Ground/ flight switch.	Ground.
76.	Brakes.	Set for taxying.			
77.	Flaps.	Up.	84.	Direction indicator.	Caged.
	On reaching dispersal.				
	Run down the engine and stop it (see para. 40).		85.	Internal control locks.	On.
78.	Ignition switches.	Off.			
			86.	Chocks.	In position.
79.	Throttle.	Fully open.	87.	Brakes.	Off.
	When the engine has stopped.		88.	Pressure- head cover.	On.
80.	Throttle.	Closed.			

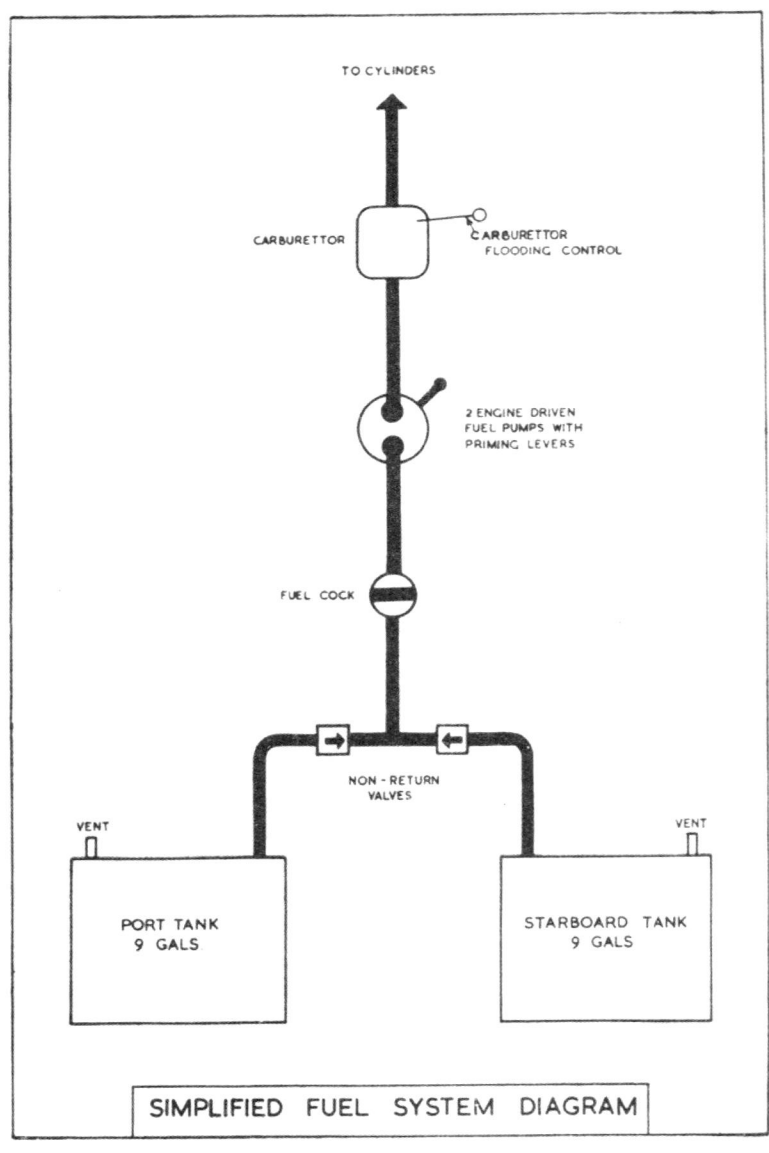

SIMPLIFIED FUEL SYSTEM DIAGRAM

PART I
DESCRIPTIVE

NOTE.—(a) The numbers quoted in brackets after items in the text refer to the illustrations in Part V.

(b) Unless otherwise stated, all speeds quoted are indicated airspeeds.

(c) Words in capital letters indicate the actual markings on the controls concerned.

1. INTRODUCTION

(i) The Chipmunk T. Mk. 10 is designed as a basic trainer aircraft and has a fixed undercarriage, fully castoring tailwheel, and totally enclosed tandem cockpits with full dual control. The leading edges of the wings and tail-plane, and the fuselage, are metal-covered ; the remainder of the wings and the control surfaces are fabric-covered.

(ii) The aircraft is powered by a Gipsy Major Mk. 8 engine, driving a fixed-pitch metal propeller, and is fitted with a self-indexing cartridge starter.

(iii) When flown solo, the pilot should occupy the front cockpit.

FUEL AND OIL SYSTEMS

2. **Fuel tanks**

Fuel is carried in two flexible 9-gallon tanks, mounted one in each wing, and is fed to the engine from both tanks simultaneously, non-return valves preventing the contents of one tank being transferred to the other. The valves also prevent the engine " cutting " if one tank is empty. Each tank is vented to atmosphere and has a ball valve which seals the vent when the aircraft is inverted.

3. **Fuel contents gauges**

A direct-reading fuel contents gauge is fitted in the top of each tank, next to the filler caps. The red figures indicate the contents when the aircraft is in the ground attitude and the white figures when in the flying attitude. In flight the gauges can only be read accurately from the front cockpit.

4 Fuel pumps and priming

(i) Two engine-driven fuel pumps are installed, and priming of the engine before starting is effected by two hand-priming levers on the fuel pumps, and by a carburettor flooder control.

(ii) The use of either of the hand-priming levers ensures that the fuel pumps, the pipeline to the carburettor and the carburettor float chamber are filled with fuel. The lever on the rear pump is fitted with an extension lever so that it may be reached and operated through an opening in the port side cowling panel.

(iii) The carburettor flooder control, which is operated by a pull wire through a second opening in the port side cowling panel, enables the carburettor to be flooded, and thus provides the required rich mixture for starting ; this is done by operating the fuel pump priming lever whilst holding out the carburettor flooding device, with the fuel cock ON.

5 Fuel cocks

A fuel cock lever (28) and (43) marked ON (fully forward) and OFF (fully back) is to the left of the base of the control column in each cockpit.

6 Oil system

The oil tank, situated forward of the bulkhead, has a capacity of 2 gallons of oil and $\frac{3}{8}$ gallons air space. A dip-stick is embodied in the filler cap, which is under the engine starboard cowling. Oil temperature gauges (15) and (45), and oil pressure gauges (16) and (46) are fitted on the instrument panel in each cockpit.

MAIN SERVICES

7 Electrical system

(i) A 24-volt electrical system is installed, and an engine-driven generator charges the aircraft batteries for the operation of the radio, the oil temperature gauges and the usual lighting services.

(ii) A master electrical switch (11) marked **GROUND** and **FLIGHT** is fitted on the port side of the front cockpit below the instrument panel and should be turned to **FLIGHT** before starting the engine. If it is left at **GROUND**, the electrical services will, after the engine is started, be running direct from the generator, and should the throttle be closed for any reason during flight, the services will fade out. The switch should be left at **GROUND** when the aircraft is parked.

(iii) An external battery socket is fitted on the port side of the fuselage for ground testing purposes. When an external battery is plugged in, the master electrical switch should be turned to **GROUND**.

(iv) A generator power failure warning light (14) is mounted in the top left-hand corner of the instrument panel in the front cockpit, and comes on when the generator is not working, if the master electrical switch is at **FLIGHT**.

8.   **Vacuum system**

An engine-driven vacuum pump is provided for working the gyro-operated flight instruments.

AIRCRAFT CONTROLS

9.   **Flying controls**

The rear control column is detachable by removing two safety pins and withdrawing two pins at its base.
The rudder pedals may be adjusted on the ground only to any of three positions, by adjusting the tube to which each pedal is secured and which is held on the rudder bar by a pin with a retaining spring clip.

10.   **Flying controls locking gear**

The flying controls locking gear consists of two rods which are fitted over the controls in the front cockpit. One hooked rod is fitted, the larger end over the left-hand end of the rudder bar and the smaller end on to the red-coloured bobbin provided on the port side of the control column base. The clip on the other rod is fitted to the control column and tightened by means of a winged nut, while the two ends are secured in spring clips on the fuselage walls.

11. Flaps control

A manually-operated flaps control lever (20) and (48) is fitted on the starboard side of each cockpit. The flaps have three positions, UP (fully forward), 15° FLAP (mid position) and 30° FLAP (fully back). To move them from the down to the mid position or from the mid to the up position, a hand-operated spring-loaded trigger fitted at the top of each lever must first be operated to release a pawl in the front cockpit quadrant. Each lever is provided with a guard to obviate accidental movement. The lever may, however, be moved from the up to the mid position or from the mid to the down position without operating the trigger.

As the flaps are easily visible from both cockpits, no position indicator is fitted.

12. Trimming tabs

An elevator trimming tab control (29) and (31), marked UP-NOSE-DOWN is on the port side of each cockpit. The control is marked so that all positions forward of " neutral " are black and all positions aft of " neutral " are white. The trimmer tab setting is read off at the top of the trimmer wheel casing. The rudder and ~~port~~ starboard aileron have fixed tabs.

13. Wheel brakes

A manually operated brake lever (10) and (39) spring-loaded in the aft position is on the port side of each cockpit. The brakes may be set at any position by pressing down on the collar on either lever, to engage a pawl on the quadrant. Slight backward movement of either lever releases the pawl so that the lever can be moved to the off position. The brakes should not be left in the fully on position when parking for long periods, as it may strain the system.

14. Throttle and mixture controls

(i) Throttle control levers (9) and (36) are fitted in quadrants on the port side of each cockpit, and each quadrant is divided into two ranges marked ECON. CRUISING and POWER JET IN.

(ii) Mixture control levers (8) and (37), are fitted on each throttle quadrant and are linked with the throttle, so that the latter cannot be closed without moving the mixture control to the " rich " (fully back) position.

(iii) Common friction nuts (7) and (38) are provided on the quadrants for both the throttle and mixture controls.

15. Air-intake heat control

Controls (24) and (47) for the air intake heat control are fitted on the starboard side of each cockpit. When the control is in the COLD (forward) position, air is fed to the engine from the duct through the engine starboard cowling. To select HOT air the control is moved aft and then down, being retained in this position by means of a slot in the front cockpit. Heated air is then fed to the engine from inside the engine cowling.

16. Engine starting controls

(i) Ignition switches (12) and (35) are fitted on the port wall in each cockpit, and both sets of switches must be on before the engine will run. The engine may, therefore, be stopped by operating the switches in either cockpit.
The magneto controlled by the starboard switches (marked No. 2) is an impulse magneto. When starting by hand the engine should be started on this magneto only, No. 1 magneto being switched on as soon as the engine fires.

L.1
ra. 16
'iD
ge 15

(ii) A self-indexing, percussion-firing cartridge starter, containing six charges, is fitted, the trigger ring control (17) being mounted in the front cockpit on the starboard side of the instrument panel. When the ring is pulled out to the full extent of its travel (approx. 9 inches) a cartridge is *both indexed and fired*.

A spring-loaded flap guard is fitted over the ring control to prevent its accidental operation. The flap should not be raised until just prior to starting.

(iii) The engine may be started if necessary by hand-swinging the propeller.

GENERAL EQUIPMENT

17. Canopy

(i) A single sliding canopy covers both cockpits and is fitted with two external handles, one for each cockpit, on the top port side of the canopy and connected to corresponding levers inside. Twisting either of the handles allows the canopy to be pulled rearwards to either of two intermediate positions in which it may be locked by releasing the handle, or to the fully open position. Handgrips are provided internally to facilitate canopy manipulation.

(ii) The canopy is not jettisonable but there is a small spring-loaded door in the roof, which assists opening, particularly at high speeds. Normally the canopy can be opened without this assistance up to a speed of 100 knots. In addition the port side panels in the canopy may be jettisoned to facilitate emergency exit (see para. 43).

18. Seats and harness

The seats are not adjustable for height. "Z" type harness (26) and (30) is provided in each cockpit.

19. Instrument flying practice equipment

(i) Amber screens, which may be fitted in flight, are stowed in a pocket (21) on the starboard wall of the front cockpit. There is one central screen hinged about the vertical centre line and provided with two fasteners for attachment to the top of the windscreen. Two side screens, which should be fitted first, are also provided, each with a single fastener, and have an approximately semicircular cut-out at the lower edge at the forward end of each screen. The lower edge of each sidescreen should be fitted into the clip at the forward end of the permanent fastener on the windscreen.

(ii) Sliding amber screens, which can only be fitted when on the ground, are on the front side panels of the canopy, and when required for use, are moved forward to join narrow amber strips which are permanently fitted at the front of the canopy.

.L.1
ara. 19
(iii)
age 17

(iii) A bag (22) for stowing the special goggles is on the front cockpit starboard wall. The ventilation socket for the goggles is also on the front cockpit starboard wall.

20. Lighting

(i) The combined switch and fuse box mounted on the front cockpit port wall has a switch (5) and a morsing push-button (6) for the identification light, the taxying lamp switch (2), the navigation lights switch (3), the front cockpit lamps OFF and dimmer switch (4) and the front cockpit emergency lamp switch (1). The compass in the front cockpit has a separate lamp and switch (27) fitted just below the compass. The emergency lamp is supplied by a small battery, independent of the aircraft electrical system, fitted just aft of the switch and fusebox.

(ii) A master switch (33) for the front cockpit lamps is mounted on the port wall of the rear cockpit and is fitted with a guard to prevent accidental operation.
Beside this switch is the OFF and dimmer switch (32) for the rear cockpit lamps, and above it the switch (34) for the rear cockpit emergency lamp which is supplied from the same battery as the front cockpit emergency lamp.
The compass in the rear cockpit also has a lamp and switch (42) fitted just below it.

21. Maps and Pilot's Notes stowage

A double stowage for maps and Pilot's Notes is mounted in front of the seat in both cockpits.

22. Baggage locker

A baggage locker is provided behind the pilot's seat in the rear cockpit.

23. Radio.

A 4-channel V.H.F. set incorporating intercommunication is fitted, and controllers (18) and (50) are mounted on the starboard side of each cockpit. In addition a selector switch (49) marked FRONT and REAR is fitted beside the rear cockpit controller. With the switch at FRONT, channel selection can only be made from the controller in the front cockpit, and with it at REAR, channel selection can only be made from the rear cockpit. Press-to-transmit pushbuttons (19) and (41), are fitted on the top of each control column, and a V.H.F. muting switch (51), for use when intercommunication only is required, is fitted aft of the rear cockpit controller.

23A. Cockpit ventilation

A ventilator is mounted in front of the windscreen, and is operated by a push-pull control at the top right-hand side of the front cockpit instrument panel. The control is marked AIR VENT—PUSH.

CHIPMUNK T10

FINAL CHECKS FOR TAKE-OFF

TRIM   ... ELEVATOR : 2 DIVS
                        NOSE HEAVY

MIXTURE   ... FULLY RICH

FUEL   ... CONTENTS

                    COCK ON

FLAPS   ... UP OR 15° DOWN

FINAL CHECKS FOR LANDING

FUEL ... CONTENTS

MIXTURE ... FULLY RICH

BRAKES ... LEVER OFF

FLAPS ... AS REQUIRED

PART II
HANDLING

24. **Management of fuel system**

The fuel cock should be set fully ON before starting, and remain in this position at all times when the engine is running. If one tank empties before the other the non-return valve in the fuel line prevents air being sucked in and causing the engine to cut.

25. **Starting the engine**

(i) After carrying out the external, internal and cockpit checks laid down in the Pilot's Checks List, items 1 to 58, confirm the following :—

Ground/Flight switch ...	FLIGHT
Fuel cock	ON
Throttle	Closed
Mixture control ...	Fully back
Air intake heat control	COLD
Ignition (front cockpit)	OFF

(ii) While the carburettor flooding device is held out, the hand priming lever should be operated through the full range of travel until fuel drips from the overflow vent at the bottom of the engine. If, due to the position of the operating cam on the pump, there is insufficient leverage on the hand priming lever, the cam position should be altered by rotating the propeller through 180°, or alternatively, the lever on the other pump, accessible from inside the cowling, may be used. The engine should not be started until fuel has ceased draining from the vent.

(iii) If the engine is cold, the propeller should be turned through about six revolutions by hand in order to prime the cylinders. A hot engine should not require priming.

(iv) Set the throttle lever about ½ inch forward from the fully closed position.

(v) Starting the engine with the cartridge starter.

(a) Switch ON both magnetos.

(b) Raise the safety flap fitted over the cartridge starter control and then pull the control to the full extent of its travel (about 9 inches). This will index and fire a cartridge. The control ring may be released immediately.

(c) The most likely cause of failure to start is over-priming. If this occurs switch OFF both magnetos, and with the throttle fully open, have the engine turned backwards by hand. If the engine still fails to start after two or three successive attempts, the cause should be investigated. In cold weather, or with a cold engine, a little additional priming may be necessary.

(vi) Starting the engine by swinging the propeller.

(a) Switch ON the impulse magneto (starboard).

(b) Have the propeller swung cleanly through the compression stroke to start the engine. When the engine is running switch on the other magneto.

(c) Over-priming should be dealt with as in (v) (c).

(vii) If the oil pressure does not rise almost immediately to 30 to 40 lb./sq. in. the engine should be shut down and the cause investigated.

(viii) Whilst warming up at 1,000-1,200 r.p.m. carry out items 59 and 60 of the Pilot's Check List.

26. **Exercising and testing**
After warming up to 30°C. oil temperature :—

(i) Test each magneto for a dead cut as a precautionary check before increasing power further.

(ii) Open up to 1,500 r.p.m. and check that the generator power failure warning light is out; then test each magneto in turn. The single ignition drop should not exceed 75 r.p.m. If it does, and there is no undue vibration, the full power check at (iii) below should be carried out. If, however, there is marked vibration, the engine should be shut down and the cause investigated.

(iii) The following full power check should be carried out after repair, inspection other than daily, when the single ignition drop at 1,500 r.p.m. exceeds 75 or at the discretion of the pilot. Except in those circumstances, no useful purpose will be served by a full power check.

(a) Open up steadily to full power and check r.p.m. which should be 2,000 to 2,100.

(b) Check each magneto in turn. If the single ignition drop exceeds 120 r.p.m. or there is excessive vibration the aircraft should not be flown.

(c) The full power check should not be unduly prolonged.

(iv) After completing the checks either at 1,500 r.p.m. or full power, steadily move the throttle to the fully closed position and check the minimum idling (approx. 650 r.p.m.), then open up to 1,000-1,200 r.p.m.

27. **Taxying**

(i) Before taxying, carry out items 61 to 63 of the Pilot's Check List.

(ii) Set the brake lever about half way back from the forward position. This will give differential braking only. A further backward movement of the lever may be required to give extra differential braking when taxying in high winds. The lever should be moved fully back when stopping the aircraft and for running up.

28. **Take-off**

(i) Carry out items 64 to 70 in the Pilot's Check List.

(ii) Align the aircraft carefully with the take-off path and then open the throttle slowly to the take-off position.

(iii) Keep straight initially by coarse use of the rudder and gentle use as speed increases. There is a tendency to swing to starboard if the throttle is opened too quickly.

(iv) The aircraft should be flown off at approximately 45 knots.

(v) At a safe height raise the flaps, if used.

29. **Climbing**

(i) The speed for maximum rate of climb is 65 knots, but 70 knots is recommended as a more comfortable speed.

(ii) Climb at full throttle. The mixture control should normally be left in the fully rich position, as a rich mixture is desirable for assistance in cooling the engine. At altitude, however, it should be moved forward only sufficiently to eliminate rough running due to over-richness.

30. General flying

(i) *Changes of trim*

    Flaps down   ...   ...   slightly nose down
    Flaps up   ...   ...   slightly nose up
There is no change of trim with operation of the canopy. Changes of power and speed promote slight changes in directional trim.

(ii) *Stability*

The aircraft is easy to trim under all conditions of flight, and holds its trimmed speed well.

(iii) *Controls*

The controls are well harmonised and the aircraft is easy and pleasant to fly. They remain light and effective throughout the speed range, except that the ailerons tend to become heavier as the limiting speed is approached.

(iv) *Flying at reduced airspeeds*

Reduce speed to 75 knots and lower 15° flap, then fly at about 65 knots. The stalling speed under these conditions is about 35 knots.

(v) *Carburettor icing*

The engine is prone to carburettor icing, which may be avoided by normal use of the air-intake heat control. Should icing occur it will be indicated by rough running or loss of power. Hot air should be selected immediately, but if in a short space of time, the icing does not clear, manipulation of the throttle lever should assist in clearing the engine.

(vi) *Mixture control*

    (a) The mixture control should be fully rich for starting, ground running and take-off. Its use in climbing and cruising flight is given in paras. 29 and 31.

    (b) Changes in altitude will require corresponding adjustments of the mixture control. It should always be returned to the fully rich position before commencing a dive.

(c) The engine should never be allowed to run for any length of time at a reduced r.p.m., where the reduction in r.p.m. is obtained by use of the mixture control.

31. Flying for range

(i) The maximum weak cruising r.p.m. are 2,300 but it is recommended that 2,100 r.p.m. are not exceeded in cruising flight. At or below 2,100 r.p.m. a weaker mixture is obtained and the possibility of rough running at the higher r.p.m. is eliminated.

(ii) The recommended range speed is 85 to 90 knots.

(iii) At the required altitude, adjust the throttle to obtain the recommended speed. The mixture control should then be moved forward towards the weak position until the r.p.m. are observed to drop or rough running commences.
It should then be moved back until the original r.p.m. and/or smooth running conditions are restored. The control will then be set in the correct position for all throttle settings at that altitude.

(iv) The recommended speed for endurance is 60-65 knots.

32. Flight planning charts

The purpose and method of use of the two charts on the following pages is fully explained in Amendment List 1 to A.P. 2095 Pilot's Notes General, 4th edition. The first chart is for cruising at 1,000 ft. and the second chart for cruising at 5,000 ft., in both cases the carburettor air intake is in the COLD position, and maximum weak mixture is obtained by the use of the mixture control (see para. 31).

NOTE.—These charts must be regarded as *provisional*. They have been compiled as the result of tests carried out on one aircraft only. Revised charts, if necessary, will be issued by amendment when further tests are completed.

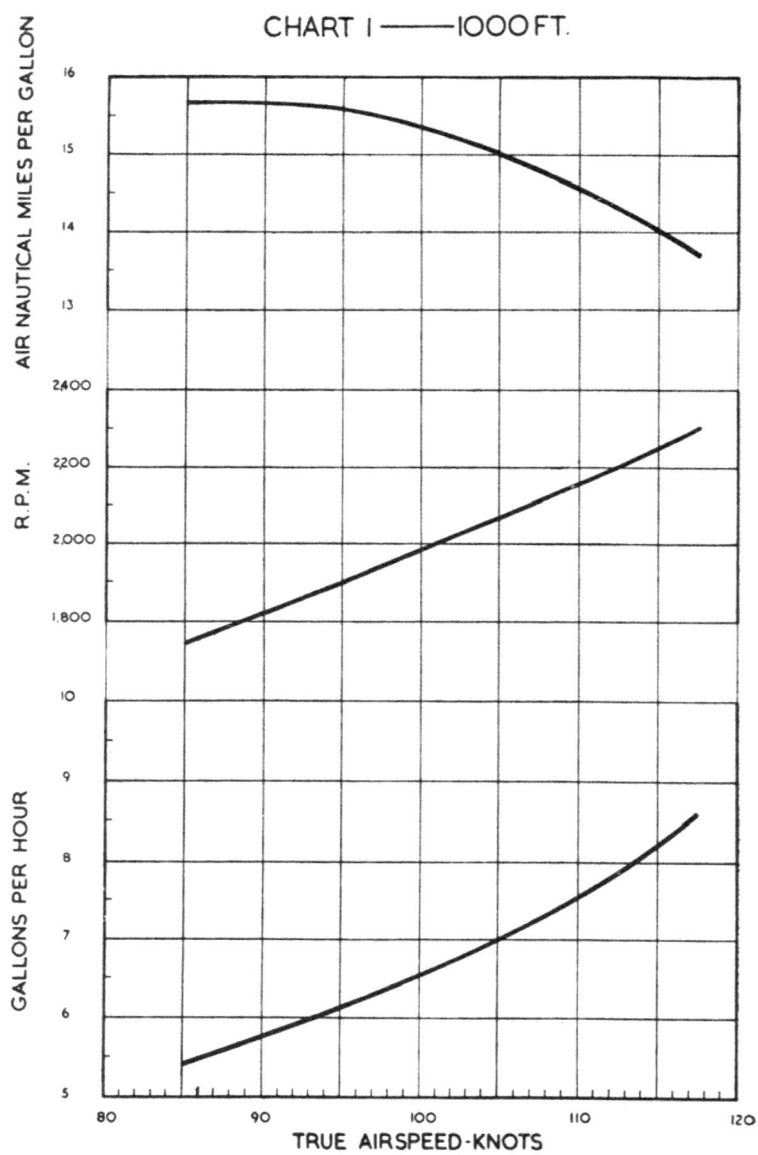

CHART I ———— 1000 FT.

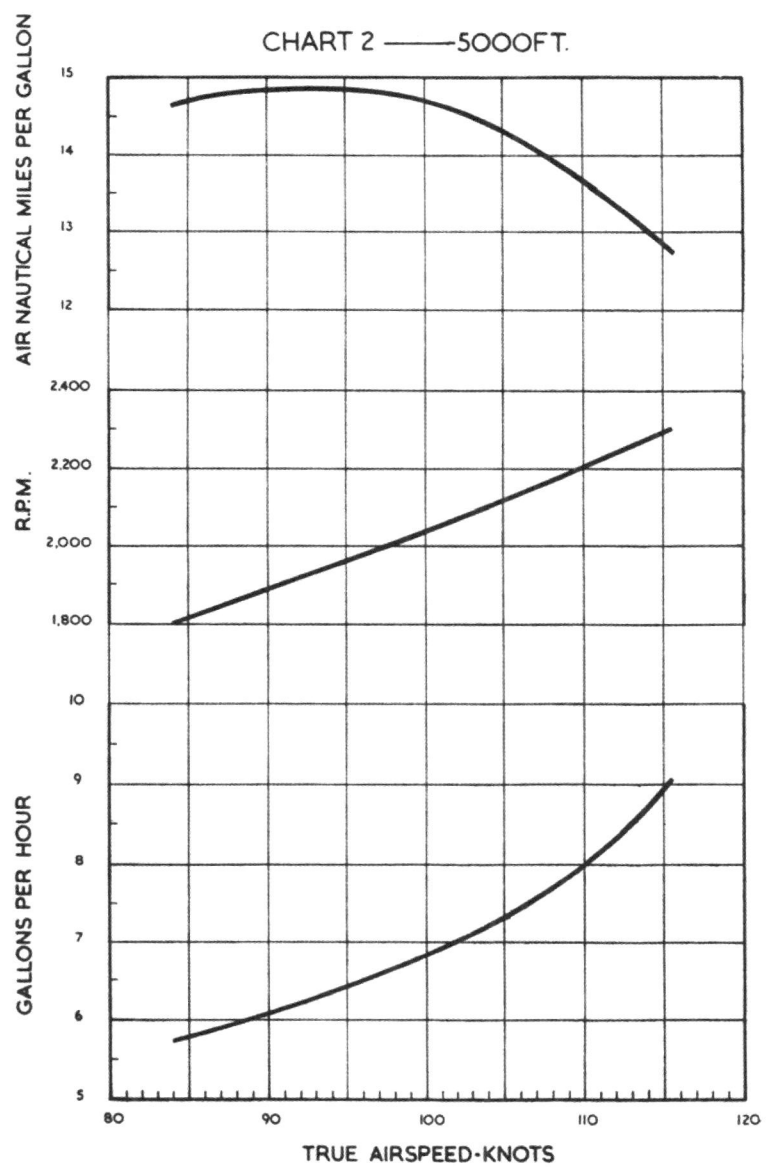

CHART 2 ————5000 FT.

33. Position error corrections

The correction for position error is as follows :—

From	..	60	66	78	94	)	
To	..	66	78	94	120	'	knots
Add	..	4	3	2	1	)	

34. Stalling

(i) The approximate stalling speeds in knots at the maximum all up weight (2,000 lb.) are : —

> *Power off*
>> Flaps up 45
>> Flaps down. 15° or 30° 35
>
> *Power on*
>> Under typical approach conditions, flaps
>> fully down 35

(ii) In all cases warning is given by slight elevator buffeting some three knots before the stall occurs. With power off, at the stall, the nose drops gently accompanied by elevator buffeting and there is a slight tendency for the nose to pitch. If the stick is held hard back. the elevator buffeting is increased and a wing will drop. With power on, the pre-stall buffeting is increased and the wing drop at the stall more pronounced.

(iii) Stalling speeds are reduced by about 2-3 knots with one pilot only in the aircraft.

(iv) With the canopy open, stalling speeds and characteristics remain unaltered.

(v) The stall in a steep turn is indicated by buffeting but there is normally no tendency to flick out of the turn.

(vi) Recovery in all cases is straightforward and easy.

35. Spinning

(i) The canopy should be closed, the flaps up and the brakes off.

(ii) The spin should be initiated with the control column held hard back, and full rudder applied in the required direction.

A L I
Para 35
(contd.)
Page 27

(iii) It may be found that the aircraft is reluctant to enter the spin, and will instead fall into a spiral dive which may easily be confused with the true spin. The spiral can be recognised by a fairly rapid rise in the airspeed, during the first two turns.

(iv) Entry into the spin can usually be facilitated by applying opposite aileron to the direction in which it is intended to spin, in addition to the normal control movement at the point of stall.

(v) Recovery is effected in the normal way by applying full opposite rudder, followed by a firm and progressive forward movement of the control column until the rotation ceases. A moderate push force is required to move the control column forward. If recovery is initiated before about 3 turns of the spin have been completed, recovery is immediate. Up to $1\frac{1}{2}$ turns may be required for recovery in the later stage when the spin is flat, or when, on the forward C.G. the rate of rotation is high.

36. Diving

(i) Before commencing the dive the mixture control should be in the fully rich position.

(ii) As speed increases the aircraft becomes progressively tail heavy, but can be held in the dive to the limiting speed without re-trimming. Directional trim should be maintained by progressive application of right rudder.

(iii) In the dive the throttle should be at least $\frac{1}{3}$ open and the use of maximum r.p.m. limited to 20 seconds. With a larger throttle opening, as the maximum speed is approached, it will be necessary to throttle back to keep the r.p.m. within the limitations.

37. Aerobatics

(i) The following speeds in knots are recommended :—

Roll	~~105-110~~ 115-120
Loop	125-130
Half roll off loop	135-140

(ii) The canopy should be kept closed during aerobatics.

(iii) For manœuvres in the looping plane, care should be taken not to exceed the r.p.m. limitations at high speed.

38. **Approach and landing**

(i) Carry out items 71 to 75 of the Pilot's Check List.

(ii) It is recommended for all conditions that the airfield boundary be crossed at a speed of 55-60 knots.

(iii) The initial glide or powered approach should be made at 60 knots.

(iv) Without the use of flap, the approach is long and flat and very little power, if any, is required.

(v) For a precautionary landing an initial approach with full flap under power at 55 knots is recommended, aiming to cross the airfield boundary at about 50 knots.

39. **Mislanding and going round again**

(i) At full throttle the aircraft will climb away easily with the flaps fully down.

(ii) Open the throttle fully and retrim if necessary. Climb at about 65 knots with the flaps lowered.

(iii) At a safe height, raise the flaps in two stages if full flap is used. There is little change of trim and no sink.

40. **After landing**

(i) Before taxying, carry out items 76 and 77 of the Pilot's Check List.

(ii) If the serviceability of the engine is in doubt, such items of the run-up given in paragraph 25 as may be necessary should be carried out. In all cases, however, the engine should be idled at 800-900 r.p.m. for a short period when the magnetos should be tested for a dead cut.

(iii) The engine should be stopped by switching off the ignition in either cockpit and opening the throttle fully.

(iv) When the engine has stopped, close the throttle and carry out the checks in the Pilot's Check List, items 80 to 88.

PART III
LIMITATIONS

41. **Engine data.** **Gipsy Major 8** (fitted with fixed pitch propeller).

	R.P.M.	Oil temp. C.
MAX. TAKE-OFF	Full throttle	85(100)*
MAX. CONTINUOUS RICH MIXTURE	2,400	85
MAX. CONTINUOUS WEAK MIXTURE	2,300	85
MAX. DIVING AT ½ THROTTLE 20 SEC. LIMIT	2,675	

OIL PRESSURE :
> Normal ... ... 40 to 45 lb./sq. in.
> Emergency minimum ... 30 lb./sq. in.

MINIMUM OIL TEMPERATURE :
> For take-off ... ... ~~+30°C~~ +15°C

* Five minutes limit.

42. **Flying limitations**

Maximum permissible diving speed ...	173 knots
Maximum speed for lowering flaps 15° and for flight with flaps lowered 15° ...	93 knots
Maximum speed for lowering flaps 30° and for flight with flaps lowered 30° ...	71 knots
Maximum permissible all-up-weight for take-off, all permitted forms of flying and landing	2,000 lb.

PART IV
EMERGENCIES

NOTE.—All emergency controls are marked with yellow and black stripes. The cockpit emergency lamp switches, however, can be identified by a luminous spot on the switch toggles.

43. **Emergency exits**

(i) The canopy is not jettisonable, but to enable it to be moved rapidly to the rearmost position in flight, the roof is fitted with a small door hinged at the rear end ; when the door is pivoted upwards, into the slipstream, it overcomes the suction of the canopy and facilitates normal opening. The door is held closed by a catch which is spring-loaded by bungee cord, and is released by pulling either of the yellow-and-black coloured knobs in the interior of the canopy on the starboard side of each cockpit.

(ii) To enable the crew to get clear or be released, in the event of the canopy being jammed in a crash, two "break-out" panels are fitted on the port side of the canopy. The operating levers for internal or external operation are marked in yellow and black stripes, and are clearly labelled showing the direction of operation.

44. **Fire-extinguisher**

A hand fire-extinguisher (23) is on the floor, on the starboard side of the front cockpit.

45. **First-aid kit**

The first-aid kit is mounted in the port mainplane near the root end and is clearly labelled. It is retained in position by a rip panel, removal of which is facilitated by a tag.

46. Crash landing

(i) Jettison the canopy side panels, leaving the canopy closed.

(ii) Tighten the safety harness and disconnect the R/T plug.

(iii) Maintain a speed of 60 knots while manœuvring with the flaps up.

(iv) Do not lower full flap until it is certain that the landing ground can be reached under full control.

(v) Make a final approach, under power if possible, at 50-55 knots.

(vi) If time permits before the touchdown turn off the fuel and switch off the ignition.

PART V—ILLUSTRATIONS